Old ANTRIM COAST

by

Sandy Watson

On Lubitavish, the hill from which this photograph was taken, golden whin bushes guard the burial chamber of the poet warrior Ossian whose ghost, legend says, has overlooked this valley since the third century. Today visitors drive between the fuschia hedgerows that grace the roadsides and head up to the site where a more recent memorial pays homage to John Hewitt, another beloved Irishman of letters. On a misty morning it's not difficult to cast your mind back to imagine the thriving community of ancient artisans who made axes on these slopes five thousand years ago. Sadly, all of the area's thatched cottages have disappeared into memory.

The publishers regret that they cannot supply
copies of any pictures featured in this book.

Printed by
Blissetts
Roslin Road
Acton
W3 8DH

Since before the Famine years, Irish cottagers have augmented the family income with the traditional handcraft of weaving. Some weavers plaited hemp rope, spun wool or embroidered delicate patterns on linen table cloths, while others, like the man pictured here, salvaged the flax 'tow' that was cast off during linen processing and wove it into simple doormats or dog beds. The giant rain barrel and makeshift water heater in this picture may have been used to soften the tow rushes or to melt the glue required to stiffen the backing. Working up until sometime in the 1940s, McCurry, a wicker of Ballyeamon, was the last full-time basket weaver in County Antrim. He boiled young hazel rods and 'sally' willow branches to make them pliable, then braided the 'whips' into baskets, donkey panniers, chair seats, and creels that had to be sturdy enough to carry hundreds of pounds of turf, fish, seaweed or potatoes over rock-strewn mountain pathways. Dan Laverty, Alec Smyth and Francis Higgerty were the last rug and tow merchants in the glens.

The Irish Peasant Home Industries sign on the right of this view of Ballycastle's Ann Street indicates the shop where instructor Stephen Clarke and German craftsman Anton Lang trained disadvantaged young men to be toymakers from 1904. The factory ceased operations in the 1930s, but the shop continued to sell crafts and souvenirs until the 1970s. On the left, in the glow of the gas light (installed in 1873) stood Coughlan's photo studio, and just a few doors away was McCahan's lending library, the post office and McCollam's bakery. Right up until the 1950s many Ulster farm families still made the journey to town by horse and cart. According to one of the last traditional cartmakers still working in Ireland, Davey George McCrory, who I interviewed during my research , 'It took two weeks to make a cart, but the first six days making the wheels were the hardest part. The knave, or the hub, was cut from elm because it was a water-repellent wood. The spokes were always oak because oak was flexible to help the suspension. The rim was ash because it was tough and durable, and we crafted that in six sections called 'fellows'. The blacksmith forged the iron hoop to cover the rim, then he made the iron axles and the hangings you see on the back of the box. The box itself was usually made of larch.'

It was landowner Hugh Boyd who established Ballycastle as a prosperous commercial centre after he bought the townland from the Earl of Antrim in 1727. He built a harbour in 1737, set up a glass factory in 1755, and also established a flour mill, colliery, brewery and salt mine in his quest to make his market town a desirable community in which to work, live and play. Summer tourists still stroll along the promenade of North Street that skirts the sandy beach. At the far end of the street, looking towards Quay Hill, can be glimpsed the last thatched house in Ballycastle. The motor car in the centre of this picture, taken in 1907, must have caused quite a stir as it conveyed owner W.H.G. Browne to the Marine Hotel all the way from his home at Orwell Park, Rathgar, Dublin. This hotel was built on the site of the former Customs House.

After war was declared in 1914 this German mine was brought ashore at Ballycastle under the direction of Coastguard Captain 'Gutty' Chamberlain who is standing in the middle of this group. From left to right, the individuals have been identified as Bobby Ferris, John Bradley, Pat McLean (farmer at Carey Mill), Johnny Coyles, Captain Chamberlain, Archie McCollum (also of Carey Mill), Francis Quigg, Frank Quigg, and well-known local athlete, Alex Jamison. Nellie Chamberlain, Gutty's daughter, is watching from a safe distance. It was not uncommon for military hardware to wash ashore in this region. Enemy ships regularly laid mines in the busy shipping routes of the North Channel, hoping to damage newly built vessels after they left the safe haven of the Glasgow shipyards.

There is an old Irish legend that tells of the Children of Lir, whose wicked stepmother turned them into swans. For 300 years they were banished to the Sea of Moyle, but some say that during winter storms they sneaked ashore for shelter near the mouth of the Margy River. Although a footbridge over the river was erected in 1895 for patrons of the Marine Hotel who wanted easier access to the nearby golf course, it was replaced in 1905 by this sturdier span constructed by the Dallat Brothers. Thereafter, everyone benefited, especially summer visitors who now had an easy route to the picnic grounds and bathing boxes at nearby Pan Rocks. Today, ramblers can stroll along a path (which partly follows the route of the tramway which was set up in 1740 by Hugh Boyd and ran from the quarry to the harbour) or wander down the strand to search for ghostly swan shapes hidden in the rock formations.

Just a half mile from Fair Head, the chaotic mass of broken basalt columns on the Grey Man's Path perch precariously 400 feet above the sea. It was said that Anfirlea, the Celtic sea god, often donned a cloak of mist and descended the path at night to bring ships to their doom. For more than 150 years, adventurers have braved the heights to pose for the camera, just as this group did for photographer Jane Cunningham, who turned the images into postcards that she sold from her shop on Ann Street in Ballycastle. The rugged landscape on this coast not only affords spectacular views, but in the past also allowed glimpses of the golden eagles which used to nest on these cliffs. After dying out decades ago, several pairs of these rare birds of prey have been reintroduced in Donegal, and conservationists hope their hunting ground will spread so that they may soon return to the north Antrim Coast.

Known locally as the 'old boat slip', the 'pool', or the 'fisherman's harbour', this jetty was a hive of activity the day this summer scene was captured. The double-ended boats are Norwegian-designed 'drontheims' owned by fishermen from Islay who regularly brought dried cod to sell at the Lammas Fair. Their masts were propped against the harbour walls and ballast stones placed on the sand while the crews went ashore. Also discernible are a few 'buckie pots' used for trapping dog-whelks for bait. In 1909 the wall on the right was erected to enclose McGildowney's pier yard. On the bank in front of the lifeboat house and smithy, several flat-ended curraghs of traditional Donegal design lie waiting for the next tide. Many blacksmiths worked double shifts as horses and carts shuttled loads from the far end of the harbour where the cargo ships and ferries docked. The coastguard officers, based in the white building in the centre, maintained a watchful eye over all.

It is an Ulster tradition to gather up the family on the last Tuesday in August and head for the 'Old Lammas Fair in Ballycastle-O' as John McAuley's popular song suggested. For hundreds of years market traders have set up stalls around the Diamond, under the O'Connor Monument, selling everything from livestock to hand-knitted jumpers, bog oak souvenirs and the frothy honeycomb toffee known locally as 'yellowman'. The fair may have begun as a clan gathering in the 1600s when the Antrim McDonnells invited their kinsmen and neighbours to participate in a festival of highland games (a tradition the family brought from Scotland), feasting and a chance to barter horses, cattle or sheep and hand-crafted products. Ballad singers would have strolled among the crowd exchanging words and music for a few coins. On the day this photograph was taken in 1946 the Royal Hotel (at the far left with the ornamental

porch roof) would have done a roaring trade; likewise, the aptly-named Corner House, and (just out of sight to the right) Malloy's pub and McKinlay's Boarding House and Restaurant. The O'Connor Monument was built in 1899 to commemorate Dr Matthew O'Connor, Medical Superintendant and Dispensary Doctor at Ballycastle Workhouse from 1844 to 1898.

Only seven miles long and two miles wide, and 'protected' by whirlpools and remarkably strong tides, Rathlin Island has been home to monks, Danish invaders, mercenaries and fishermen for centuries. Perhaps its most famous visitor was Robert the Bruce who is said to have taken shelter in a Rathlin cave after his defeat in 1306; this was where he observed the famous spider which inspired him not to give up his fight for Scottish independence. That same spirit of commitment among the local Irish speakers has kept many cultural traditions alive, such as dancing 'set' quadrilles and 'Waves of Tory' during winter ceilidhs. In 1901 Marconi conducted the earliest radio telephone experiments in the UK from his wireless station on the island.

In 1746 Reverend John Gage bought Rathlin Island from the fifth Earl of Antrim. The long low building in the middle of this photograph housed the weavers' cottages which were built by Gage for the talented craftsmen and -women he found on the island. The large warehouse on the right was a storage shed for the wool and finished products which Gage sold on the mainland on behalf of the residents. After developing this sustainable industrial community, Gage erected the Manor House, stables, walled garden and orchard in 1760.

It was a six-mile return trip to Rathlin from Ballycastle for the mailboat, longer in bad weather, but a necessary journey. With no fuel on the island, peat had to be transported in addition to the post and various provisions. When this photo was taken in the late 1920s, the Coyle family operated the mailboat. Today, the Manor House is a hotel operated by the National Trust and a daily water transport service conveys residents and tourists to and fro on a regular timetable. Visitors flock to the island during the summer months for bird-watching holidays, hiking, picnics, and outdoor activities.

One glance into the River Dunn at Cushendun is sufficient to see how the peaty hillsides leaking into this burn have given the brown water its Irish name. In 1903 this bridge was partially washed away during a flood which caused extensive damage after heavy rains dislodged soil and debris high up on the moss and washed this downstream. Situated twelve miles south-east of Ballycastle, the village of Cushendun boasts a mile-long strand of sandy shore that has attracted artists and literary figures such as John Masefield and the Irish poet Moira O'Neill, who penned her famous 'Songs of the Glens of Antrim' at Rockport, her beachfront house overlooking this bay. 'Peace & Plenty', the stalwart vessel on the left, began service as a lifeboat on the Isle of Man before being purchased by the Finlay family who converted her for coastal fishing. Several generations of Cushendun fishermen plied the local waters in this boat, netting bountiful catches of salmon and cod before she was sold to the owner of the Isle of Sanda off the south coast of Kintyre.

Just a mile south-west of Cushendun, the peaceful haven of Knocknacarry has charmed generations of visitors. In the far background the two-room village school was built in 1850, while the Royal Irish Constabulary headquarters stands just out of sight to the right of the large tree. You can still see the steps used by the police to mount their horses, although the barracks have since been converted into a private home. The low buildings on the right once housed a blacksmith's premises before becoming the dwelling places they are today. In 1888 Mrs I. Kennedy was grocer/postmistress in the shop on the left; this later became McKay's grocery shop and is now a dwelling. Behind that, one of O'Hara's carts can be seen, perhaps having just returned from a run to Parkmore where it regularly transported goods and passengers from the Belfast & Northern Counties Railway terminus to the seaside communities of the Antrim coast.

Born in Glenarm, Henry 'Knockemdown' McNeill had such an entrepreneurial spirit that he won the contract for the first horse-car mail service between Carrickfergus and Ballyclare before he reached the age of eighteen. By the time he was sixty he owned seven hotels, 200 horses, hundreds of carriages, a tour company, and a collection of specially built motor-driven charabancs like the one in this picture. In the late 1920s, it was estimated that McNeill charabancs transported 1,000 passengers a day on the Portrush to Portstewart route alone. Always on the lookout for unique opportunities, McNeill purchased Garron Tower, the stately home of Lord and Lady Londonderry, and in 1899 turned it into the premier hotel north of Belfast. Only the year before he had founded the Larne Tourism Development Association and spearheaded a committee to print and distribute 20,000 copies of a booklet extolling the virtues of visiting the Antrim Coast, an innovative concept, now known as 'destination marketing' but unheard of at that time.

Shore Road, Cushendall, *c.*1940. When Francis Turnley, a son of local gentry and a philanthropist, purchased Cushendall after returning from service with the East India Company, he erected the 45 foot high Curfew Tower around 1809. A spring-fed well on the ground floor supplied the town with its water via a fountain on the east wall. The 1880 *Bassett's Directory* states that the five-storey red-sandstone tower contained a 'lock-up and guard house'. Dan McBride, and later Bernard Murphy, lived there rent free in exchange for ringing the curfew bell at 9 p.m. nightly. William Makepeace Thackery, in his 1843 *Irish Sketchbook*, praised the 'fresh boiled bacon and small beer for 8d' available at the Cushendall Inn and, while the inn is now a

hardware shop, visitors still stop on the street to purchase sweets and locally made souvenirs. One of Shore Road's best-loved businesses was the Cushendall Toy Making Factory, a hive of activity during the Edwardian era, when exquisitely crafted 'galloping horses, dolls' houses, and miniature jaunting cars' were shipped from here to customers all over the world. On the left a Coast Road motor coach passes the Northern Bank Company building which was erected in 1914. Tourists still throng to Cushendall during the summer for bathing, golfing, sailing, traditional culture at the annual Glens' Feis, and for the All Ireland Hurling Championship finals.

Today, the town remains much the same as when this photograph of Bridge Street was taken in the late 1930s. The majestic beech and sycamore trees in the background, reportedly planted when Queen Victoria ascended the throne in 1837, were a gift to the town from Francis Turnley.

Cushendall residents point with pride to the fact that their town was the first small community in Ireland to be lit by electricity. This generating station was built in 1923, according to a plaque still visible on the side of what is now Henry McKillop's Garage. The electricity was generated by the same mill race on the River Dall that had been powering Turnley's corn mill (in the centre of the picture) since 1830.

The petrol pump and white building in the centre (once a bathhouse) were removed in the 1970s to construct an entrance to a new riverside car park. In that location two blacksmiths' shops and a saddler also conducted business. The sign advertising Delargy's Hotel referred to a grand edifice that once graced the opposite side of this corner. Built by a sea captain, grandfather of the first Professor of Irish Folklore at University College, Dublin, the hotel was later owned by Mrs M. Black, then Miss E. Bradley, and finally by Mr and Mrs D. Patrick, before it was destroyed by a bomb during the Troubles. Knockmoy Fold currently occupies that site.

A quiet view of Mill Street with Kate and Lilly Morrison's drapery shop on the right with Dan McAllister's auction house adjacent. Just down the street Rosina's sold sweets, Hugh McSparron had a flesher's shop, and Joe McCollum operated a pub. Old timers still remember those who made their living on the left side of this street: Mrs Anderson with her Temperance Hotel; Mullan, the butcher; W. McFettridge, the saddler, whose brother Billy owned the garage behind the petrol pump; McCormick's grocery; Charlie Hamill's bakery; Duffy's boarding house, Mort's Transport and Parcel Post Agency; McCambridge's taxi; and Murphy's grocery. Cushendall's old courthouse, just out of sight in the background, was such a classic building it was dismantled and rebuilt at Cultra Folk Park. In the background is the Market Yard (which earlier had been used as a cinema), across from the present tourism office.

Outdoor enthusiasts always appreciated the botanical information provided by knowledgeable guides, such as Jerry, who shepherded groups along the forest trails that meandered through Glenariff Park. At the lower end of the park, on the other side of this rustic bridge, visitors were enchanted by Laragh Lodge, a picturesque wooden tea house complete with thatched roof and coloured panes of glass through which the cascading waterfalls shimmered. In springtime the rock pools became a magnet for amateur photographers, attracted by the scent of wild garlic that drifted over the nodding bluebells and the breathtaking vista of emerald green shamrocks. Both the tea house and bridge have been replaced by modern structures.

Although legend says 'the tears of the mountain' were magically conjured up by 'the little people', for more than a century visitors (of all shapes and sizes) to Glenariff have followed the sound of water plunging over the granite cliffside to find these enchanting cascades shrouded in rainbow-hued mists. In the Edwardian era four trains a day brought day-trippers from Belfast and beyond to Parkmore Halt. Enterprising wagoners waited at the lodge below the falls, offering an alternative route home via the foot of the glen and along the Coast Road to Larne railway station. Today, this beauty spot in Glenariff, the 'Queen of the Glens', continues to attract sightseers and naturalists who come to savour the tranquillity of an unspoiled wilderness.

It was the development of iron ore mining in the hills above Glenravel in 1866 that precipitated the construction of the narrow gauge Ballymena, Cushendall & Red Bay Railway for the transportation of the ore. This made Parkmore, opened in 1876 and 1,850 feet above sea level, one of the highest railway stations in the UK. In 1889 the Belfast & Northern Counties Railway Company revitalised the line, which had been closed when the mining ended, by asking B.D. Wise to design a network of woodland walkways through Glenariff Park, culminating at the spectacular waterfalls. This innovative project established a unique tourism destination that soon justified a new passenger service. In the summer of 1902 a First Class Day Trip excursion ticket from Belfast to Parkmore cost 7/6, with many passengers choosing to return by motor coach along the Coast Road via Larne for a refreshing change of scenery. The Parkmore post office and shop were managed by Maggie Millar for almost half a century until the rail line closed in 1940. The building is now a dwelling.

What is the mysterious cargo about to be shifted by this coal-burning road locomotive, capable of pulling a 40-ton load? The location appears to be the natural harbour at Garron Point, just north of Carnlough, and the mast in the background and downward sloping ramp indicate the object is being offloaded from a sailing ship. Three men are standing on what seems to be a wooden ammunition box and the block and tackle on the derrick has been wound twice to enable the pulley system to handle weights of 15 to 20 tons. These clues suggest that the heavily battened object is part of a field gun about to be transported to nearby Garron Tower, which held a temporary military garrison at the advent of the First World War. The steamroller probably came from Gregg's, a successful Larne haulage contractor who owned fifty similar engines at that time.

More than 100 years after this picture was taken, hikers walking the Ulster Way over the distant plateau above Garron Point are still mesmerised by the sight of Waterfoot village nestling at the mouth of the Glenariff River where it flows into Red Bay. On the far shore, beneath the plateau, a terrace of miners' cottages overlooks the remains of the pier where iron ore was loaded onto ships from a tiny railway that operated in the 1870s. Not far to the right of the terrace is the cemetery where a chapel was erected in 1837 (and replaced in 1917). The enterprising McAuley family, owners of the shop and post office beside the bridge, thrived as grocers, wool buyers, livestock salesmen, and auctioneers for 120 years. Their shop is now a dwelling. Behind the ruined shell on the right lived the Murray brothers, divers and marine salvage experts who made their living scouring shipwrecks, including the Belgian royal yacht *Clementine*, which sank in the bay during the First World War. During the Second World War stones from the ruin on the right were used by the armed forces to make barricades to protect this easily accessible shoreline.

Named after the colour of the rock in this iron-rich region, the Red Arch tunnel at Red Bay was one of the engineering challenges facing William Bald who supervised construction of the Antrim Coast Road in the 1830s. When the project started, the budget was £18,000, but ten years later the final cost had rocketed to £37,266. Hidden in the cliffside to the left of this photo is a series of caves which have served as dwelling places for centuries. During the building of the road, Bald set up a blacksmith's forge in one of these natural formations. In another of the caverns, archaeologists discovered a skeleton, stone axes and coins dating back to AD 839 when Danes and Vikings occupied this shoreline. In the mid-nineteenth century a 100 year-old woman, known locally as Nanny (full name Ann Murray), made her home in the largest cave and took advantage of passing traffic by selling refreshment to travellers. In an ingenious ploy to get around the licensing laws of the time she sold water by the glass while a drop of her whiskey was free. Perched on the promontory above this arch are the crumbling ruins of Red Bay Castle, built by the McDonnells of Antrim on the site of a former Norman motte and bailey, and destroyed by Cromwellian soldiers in 1652.

Judging by the chalky outcroppings on this section of the Coast Road, these pedlars are *en route* between Carnlough and Waterfoot. In 1817 Rev. Stewart Dobbs wrote, 'The road from Carnlough to Red Bay is very hilly. From the Point, the road lies through limestone rocks that have fallen from the hill upwards of 800 feet high, so that in a winter storm a traveller is exposed to stones from above, the spray of the sea beneath, and the risk of slipping, in some spots of the road, from pressure of clay under his feet. The road has gradually been improved and even now numbers of travellers pass this way to the Giant's Causeway . . .' For decades this section of the road was plagued by highwaymen who took advantage of the blind curves and isolated location to rob travellers, then escape into the steep, almost impassable hills where they could find refuge in 'hidden' villages such as Galboley. Even by the late 1800s, particularly in such remote regions of the glens, it was not unusual to find carts with traditional solid wooden wheels like those of early Celtic chariots. The carts in this photograph feature spoked 'Scots wheels' which turn independently on the axle.

Judging by the commotion on the judges' boat in the background, a shotgun is about to sound the warning signal for the start of another race during Carnlough's Regatta Day. With an excellent harbour and long seafaring tradition, Carnlough's menfolk have always taken to the waves for pleasure or profit. Whenever the merchant navy held a recruiting drive during the Second World War, a rally at Carnlough Harbour guaranteed a fully subscribed contingent. Since the first regatta in 1871, water sports have brought together all sectors of the community in a spirit of harmony, good seamanship, and fun. The classic clinker-built vessel on the far left is 'The Violet', although only two members of the legendary McCambridge rowing team are at the oars. With a reputation for building and racing swift gigs, Carnlough crews have won a host of All Ireland trophies over the past 125 years and they still ensure sailors of all ages have a chance to shine, with categories for under-12s and honoured veterans. Every December, a Harvest of the Sea service is held here to pay tribute to mariners whose lives have been dedicated to the deep.

In 1801 Philip Gibbons, a former sea captain and wealthy landowner, funded construction of a pier to protect Carnlough's natural harbour from the constant onslaught of rough seas. Providing a safe haven for ships over 20 tons meant limestone quarried above Carnlough could be safely shipped to markets across the North Channel. In 1854 the Marchioness of Londonderry saw the need to dredge the harbour entrance, repair decaying piers, extend rail access from the quarry to the harbour, and build a dockside coalyard. Soon the village had a fully employed workforce, as well as a motley crew of young 'wharf rats', like the boys in this photograph, who spent their days harbourside watching sailors scale high rigging, fishermen deliver cod, clams and flounder, Scottish freighters discharge coal, and weighmasters record limestone shipments bound for Liverpool. Soon Lady Londonderry's summer guests were also mooring their private yachts here, adding a dash of colour to the bay. Many sea captains enjoyed their brief visits to this port so much that they returned to retire here, prompting the village fathers to name one of the streets as Skipper's Row.

Built in 1854 by local stonemason Patrick Mahon, under the direction of the Marchioness of Londonderry, this building in Carnlough served as a town hall, meeting place and community concert hall for years before the ground floor was converted for use as a library in 1983 (the upper rooms are no longer accessible). Mail coaches such as the one in the picture left the nearby Londonderry Arms Hotel for twice-daily trips up and down the Antrim Coast Road. The signal board on the bridge was used by crews sending railway wagons carrying limestone from the local quarry to the harbour where a turntable and chute system provided easy access to waiting boats. Carnlough Harbour, built by Lady Londonderry to help the local economy during the Famine years, prospered for almost a century, but nowadays only a small fleet of fishing boats and pleasure craft use the sheltered anchorage.

A thriving Presbyterian congregation still holds Sunday meetings in this charming old church (or 'hall' as it was called) which was built in 1892, but the house and shop next door have seen several incarnations since this picture was taken around 1917. The dwelling place was designed and built by John Langtree, land steward for Lady Londonderry from 1843 to 1850. Part of the ground floor was converted to a shop operated by the Nicholls family before it became a general store owned by the Johnstons. It was then a café operated by the Harrison sisters and is now Killough's pharmacy.

For more than a century, cutting-edge British industries paid the humble kelp gatherers of the Antrim Coast £5 per ton to provide the key ingredient in the manufacture of soap, bleach, glass, dyes, salt and antiseptic. Locals collected seaweed from March until June, dried the 'tangles', then dug troughs about 15 feet long by 2 feet deep into which gorse branches were piled for fuel. The dried 'wrack' was then spread over iron bars and the fire lit underneath. Acrid white smoke from these shore-side fires burned day and night until all that remained was ash which hardened to a solid mass when cooled. The end product was shipped across the sea where it was transformed into iodine and silver iodide which was widely used in photographic processing, X-ray photography, and a host of other applications. Kelp merchants such as Dobbs (recorded in 1817), McAlister (1856), and Paterson (1868) provided work for the harvesters, but it was Alex Crawford in the early 1900s whose keen marketing techniques breathed new life into this old tradition and provided fairer payments to the suppliers. Nowadays, the only fresh seaweed bought and sold in this region is the distinctive savoury snack known as dulse.

In the centre of this photograph of the Square, taken around 1930, the bell on Dan Martin's pony-driven ice-cream cart signals a welcome chance for refreshment. With the bus stop, public toilets and waterfront esplanade just across the street, this section of the Antrim Coast Road has always been busy; but during the annual regatta visitors from as far away as Scotland have flocked to enjoy the festivities. Behind McAuley's Hotel and pub, a bicycle repair shop and garage also served generations of travellers. On the far left, just out of view, coach passengers from places such as Dublin would insist on stopping for tea or a meal at Smith's Dining Rooms overlooking the bay. Rebuilt after a fire in 1912, McAuley's is still open and its reputation for hospitality goes back centuries to when it sheltered United Irishmen who had dispersed after their 1798 uprising. In 1827 it also took in survivors from the wreck of a ship, *The Enterprise*.

No matter how much rock was blasted, smoothed and fashioned into sturdy seaside perimeter walls, bad weather, avalanches and constant use sometimes caused damage to the surface of William Bald's Coast Road. Perhaps the horse leading the bakery cart in the background bolted at the sight of two bicycles rounding this bend, but no matter what the cause it's unlikely these cyclists injured more than their pride in the mishap. In 1849, not far from this section of the Coast Road near Carnlough, Lady Londonderry asked her agent, John Lanktree, to erect a stone tablet as a remembrance of the Famine which had recently passed. It was inscribed with the following words: 'Frances Anne Vane, Marchioness of Londonderry, being connected with this province by the double ties of birth and marriage and being desirous to hand down to posterity an imperishable memorial of Ireland's affliction and England's generosity in the year of 1846–47, unparalleled in the annals of human suffering, hath engraved this stone.'

Photographed walking through Glenarm's Altmore Street around 1867, a sailor passes a group of barefoot children playing marbles on the dirt road. With a fine natural harbour, reportedly good enough for King John to have landed on its shore in 1206, Glenarm Bay has been home port to many a mariner. In the background is the shop of William Blackwood Pullin who sold jewellery and clocks before his daughter married R.N.Green, who retired from the Royal Navy to make homemade ice cream which he sold by horse and cart throughout the countryside. A former sailor, he opened a second shop on the Coast Road, added a tearoom and garden, and offered customers a chance to while away a Sunday afternoon dancing on the lawn to the music from an old Victrola phonograph player. The building on the far left, at the foot of the Vennel, was once a bank, but is now a jewellery workshop where visitors can watch delicate gold and silver objects being created by hand.

The distinguished gentleman holding the telescope on the left of this photograph from around 1900 is Captain Farnham Green who had command of Glenarm Coastguard Station from 1894 until 1904. According to the 1899 *Ulster Directory* his crew included J. Stoure, Wm. Thomas Portland, Charles Cook (Chief Boatman), and W. West. The 1901 census lists the men assigned to Glenarm Station as Boatmen G.A. Murlow and W. Merritt, aged 28 and 29 respectively. Like modern volunteer firefighters, many villagers worked as auxiliaries and part-timers to man the boat station on the landward side of the Coast Road. A small slipway on the seaward side provided access for the lifeboat. Recently refurbished, the village's harbour was once visited by sailing ships and coastal steamers which were loaded with limestone from the local quarry, iron ore from mines in the glen and 'chalk' (powdered limestone for use as an additive to white paint) from the local whitening mill. Glenarm Coastguard Station was closed after the Second World War and the cottages that had housed the staff since 1896 were converted into private homes.

This row of tenement houses (known as Brick Row) on Mark Street, built during the reign of Queen Victoria for the employees of Lord Antrim of Glenarm Castle, has now been demolished and replaced by Castle View Cottages. However, Alex O'Boyle, now in his nineties, still remembers many of the families who called the row home. 'The Russells, Irvines, McDowells, Charlie McClelland . . . a lot of the folks liked to keep a cow for milk in them days, but them houses were only one room and a kitchen. So they'd tether their cow up Knockanar (the brae behind) in good weather and bring the crathur down into the kitchen at the first blowin' o' snow.' A collection of small businesses thrived across the road, some in the dwelling places, just out of sight. Attie McGavock operated a tailor shop in an upstairs bedroom of his house, while Mrs Mulvenna reared pigs and turkeys in the shade of a large tree in her backyard and Mrs Dempsey sold sweets and tea from a couple of shelves in her front hallway. On the beach, just out of sight across the Coast Road (left of the picture), was a freshwater well. James Balmer remembers a time when, if the tide was low, you could have filled a cup with fresh water there. 'That wee well was just below the Whistlewood trees. You could cut a twig from a branch o' them trees, strip off the bark, dig out the middle, then you coulda' poked a wee hole and blown it like a whistle.' That grove of trees still shades the end of Mark Street today.

The land surrounding Glenarm Castle had such vast forest reserves that foresters were employed to manage the woodlots. During the 1860s a sawmill was established on the estate to cut the timber into a variety of saleable commodities. Lumber sale account books record a steady trade in fence post palings, firewood, and boards for making carts, sheds, furniture and houses. From 1898 to 1903 a small factory was set up deep in the estate's deer park by R. Hutchinson, a Scottish clog merchant who purchased a stand of larch trees from Lord Antrim and set up an operation to hew and dry 'forms' for making wooden shoes. In the late 1930s, under the direction of Lady Angela, Countess of Antrim, a furniture factory bustled with activity in the old laundry building behind the castle, producing beautifully crafted cabinets and wardrobes. The huge crosscut saw in this photograph from 1901 can still be seen on display in the walled garden of the castle during open days every July.

Cutting turf 'up on the moss' was a necessity for most families in the Antrim glens at the turn of the twentieth century because they were dependent upon the peat for cooking and heating throughout the entire year. First the peat had to be 'footed' or 'castled' (propped in small stacks) until it dried. Then the 'trinkets' were heaved onto wooden slipes, wheelbarrows, or into creels on the backs of donkeys, so they could be carried down 'off the mountain' to be stored near the house for the winter. A freshly cut clod of waterlogged peat often weighs as much as 15 pounds, but it will shrink by up to an eighth of this weight when dried. Cutting and transporting peat was backbreaking work, but when the locals huddled by the hearth on a cold winter night, warming their toes and savouring the sweet 'reek of the peat', the reward was better than gold. Though many homes now have central heating, you can still find farms, like the one near Glenarm where this photograph was taken, where the distinctive old-world scent still wreaths the kitchen and wafts up the chimney

Men have perched on the bridge parapet at the foot of Toberwine Street for more than 130 years, but nowadays their discussion would probably be interrupted by the grinding gears of coaches and lorries negotiating the tight roundabout corner as they head up the busy Coast Road. Judging by the new telegraph pole in the background, this photograph must date from 1871. Note the leather apron on the working man standing facing the camera, a garment usually worn by a blacksmith or saddler. In the Glenarm section of the 1868 *Ulster Directory* no blacksmith is listed, but James Lusk, who lived on Toberwine Street, is identified as the village saddler. In the background, a surfaceman rakes the dirt road in front of the old Heather Dew Bar, now called the Poacher's Pocket. When heavy rains are accompanied by high tides, the mouth of the Glenarm River has been known to overflow to flood neighbouring buildings, a problem which has afflicted the area around the bridge ever since it was built in 1823.

Policemen of the Royal Irish Constabulary outside the Agent's House on Altmore Street. The agent, or land steward, collected rent, accepted petitions, and negotiated turf-cutting and tree-cutting rights on behalf of the Earl of Antrim. Before the Glenarm courthouse was constructed, this section of the building housed the original Manor Court, complete with a holding cell which still has iron bars on the windows. This photograph, part of the private Holden Collection of photographs taken between 1867 and 1871, gives an insight into the uniforms and weaponry adopted in the post-Crimean War period. Going along from left to right, the sub-inspector wears a soft pillbox hat with no harp or crown (these were added in September 1867); the bearded trooper carries a cavalry sword issued by his mounted division; the next man has four chevrons and a crown on his sleeve to denote the rank of head constable 2nd class; the tall fellow with three gold chevrons is a constable (although in 1884 this mark of rank was applied to sergeants only); and the acting constable has two gold chevrons. The five men of lower rank on the right side of the line appear to be wearing trousers in a rough fabric known as 'kusey' and double-peaked 'shakos' with the Order of the Star of Bath, surmounted by the Hanoverian crown. The troop is armed with Enfield percussion rifles with sword bayonets (curved blades), issued in the early 1860s.

On the beachfront of the busy Antrim Coast Road just north of Larne, Ballygalley Café has always been a magnet for summer visitors who fancy an ice cream on a hot sunny day. Even when the wind ruffles the waves in the bay and storm clouds brood over Scawt Hill, passers-by like to stop for 'a wee scoot o' tea and a scone'. The car park entrance behind the sign leads to a busy area which on Sundays in July and August draws people from many miles around for open-air church services. Just behind, the former Coastguard cottages, built in the 1860s, sit facing the Maiden's Lighthouses (erected in 1828).

A post office is central to any village and Ballygalley's still serves as the local information exchange with a bulletin board announcing news of interest to residents. An 1888 directory listed Miss Catherine McAuley as the village postmistress. The White House Café was originally the main Coastguard station before it became the post office and then the café. It has now been converted into a private dwelling, while the current post office is still in the premises it occupies in the picture. Always popular as a summer resort, the village has grown in recent years with modern additions spreading over farmland and hillsides. Developers digging foundations for the new houses are constantly reminded that the name Ballygalley means 'townland of the rocks'.

A day at Ballygalley Bay in 1937, when this photograph was taken, meant Mother was dressed in silk stockings and high heeled shoes, Father lounged on the sand in a suit, shirt and tie, Granny wore a long coat and hat, and the children scampered about in knitted bathing costumes. In the background the outline of a face can be clearly seen on Ballygalley Head. On the tiny islet just offshore there still stands the ruins of a tower which dates from the seventeenth century and is known as O'Halloran's Tower after the location became the fictional home of a character of that name created in 1820 by Larne novelist James McHenry. In the Victorian era an old hermit known as Marina Jane eked out a meagre living on the strand by gathering, drying and selling dulse. For years she lived in a ramshackle dwelling made of driftwood, stones and moss, despite the efforts of local residents to provide her with more substantial shelter further inland. Tragically, she was washed out to sea and drowned during a cyclone in December 1894.

Ballygalley Youth Hostel was the first post-war hostel to be designed and built by the Youth Hostel Association of Northern Ireland (with generous grants from the South African Aid to Britain Fund and the Ministry of Education). The facility was opened in 1957 by their Royal Highnesses, the Duke and Duchess of Gloucester, along with the Governor of Northern Ireland, Lord Wakehurst. Situated on an elevated position overlooking the bay, the hostel provided dormitory accommodation plus a camping ground, but in the mid-1990s deterioration forced closure of the site. However, the site was bought in 1997 by Mr David Magill who renovated and reopened it as Ballygalley Holiday Apartments, offering tourists award-winning self-catering facilities.

In 1899 publican Bernard McQuillan, of the Halfway House at Ballygalley, advertised 'Nothing but the best brands of liquor supplied. Tourists are recommended to call'. And so they did, by the coachload. This 1931 photograph shows a typical summer weekend afternoon when charabancs and touring cars overflowing with punters stopped for petrol and a welcome spot of refreshment on their way up or down the Antrim Coast Road. With this guaranteed trade, ice cream vendors often set up stalls to tempt road-weary travellers. This hotel, bar and restaurant is now owned by former world flyweight boxing champion, Dave McAuley.

Built in 1625 by James Shaw of Greenock, Scotland, the fortified Scottish baronial style Ballygalley Castle, complete with turrets, gatehouse and dungeon, is now a thriving hotel. Two buildings sit directly opposite on the seafront. The taller, white edifice was a barn and beside it was a farm field. Today, a car park has replaced both. In the eighteenth and nineteenth centuries the lower building in the foreground was a boathouse for the castle. It is now leased as a craft shop during the summer.

A little detective work in the motor vehicle registration records has revealed that the car in this picture was owned by W. Ceasar Calcough who lived at 2 Fairfield Park, Rathgar, County Dublin. Mr Calcough's 1905 journey up the Antrim Coast Road may have been temporarily interrupted by this mishap, but it looks as if the sunshine was warming the seat of his Humberette and the colour and scent of the fuschias would no doubt have remained in his memory as he continued on his way.